The Children's Book of ADVENT QUESTIONS

★ THE CHILDREN'S BOOK OF ★
ADVENT QUESTIONS

Copyright © 2023 Mellani Day
All Rights Reserved.
Breaking Well Media, LLC
Colorado, U.S.A.
Design by Crystal Studios
Graphics Generated with AI

ISBN (Print): 979-8-218-30987-3
ISBN (eBook): 979-8-218-30988-6

www.breakingwellmedia.com

December 1

WHY WAS JESUS BORN?

At the beginning of time, Adam and Eve lived in the garden of Eden. They had a special relationship with God their father who created them. They visited with Him every day. But one day they chose to go against God. They ruined that special relationship and by doing that also ruined the world God had created. Sin entered the world. Adam and Eve were so sorry for themselves and for all of us born afterwards.

God decided to someday make everything good again. So He created a plan to repair what went wrong way back then. God's plan was to send Jesus into the world through this birth that we celebrate at Christmas. Jesus, a very part of God, agreed to do it, and when the time was right, God sent Jesus to come to earth as a baby. So now while we wait for all people to be born that will be born from the past, present and into the future, we celebrate his birth every year. And we look forward to living with him in a perfect world someday. And it will be even better than before.

December 2

How Can a Baby Be King, Messiah, and Save the World?

There are many prophesies in the Bible that told about the coming Messiah who would be king and what was going to happen when he came to save the people. Jesus, who was with God from the beginning of the world, agreed that he would do something to save all the people from that sin and separation from God.

The sin was passed down from Adam to everyone that has ever been born. But to undo the sin, the baby that was going to be the Messiah, had to be born outside of that sin. So, God worked a miracle and sent Jesus to be born as a baby to Mary. He was not under the curse of sin so when he grew up and accomplished his work as the Messiah, he could beat sin and save the world! That is how this baby could be Messiah, save the world, and someday be King.

December 3

Where Did Mary, Who Would Be Mother of Jesus, Live?

You might think that Mary who became the mother of Jesus, would live in a castle and be a great queen that God chose to accomplish his plan for earth. But that is not the case.

We know that baby Jesus was born in a manger in Bethlehem after Mary and Joseph traveled there. But before that, Mary lived in a simple house in a town called Nazareth. That is where Jesus eventually grew up. Mary was a traditional Jewish girl with a traditional family, and she was ready to serve God.

The angel told her she would bear a son who would save the world and someday be king of kings. She realized that God's plan would mean this king would be raised, not in a castle, but in a humble home.

December 4

What Did Mary Think?

Mary was a young Jewish woman who was engaged to be married to a man named Joseph. One day an angel came and said to her, "Mary, you are going to have a baby who will be the son of God." Mary could not understand because she was a virgin. But God who created all things could make it happen and the angel told her so. Mary loved God so she opened her heart and life to this plan that God had for her. It changed her life forever.

December 5

What Did Mary Do After She Found Out That She Was Going to Have a Baby?

Mary was engaged to be married to Joseph, a good and respected man. After the angel told her she would have a baby and that came to be, she went to Joseph her fiancée and told him about the angel's message from God and that she was pregnant with God's son. It was such an unbelievable story that Joseph actually thought that Mary was lying to him. Joseph thought that he would break off the engagement and was so sad. But as he was planning to do that, the angel visited him as well and told him that what Mary said was true. She was pregnant with God's son and that Joseph was to raise him as his own and call him Jesus. That name means "to rescue". Jesus would rescue all the people from their sins and restore them to God.

December 6

WHO WAS JESUS' COUSIN?

Another thing Mary did when she knew she was pregnant with God's son, was to go and visit her cousin Elizabeth. Elizabeth was also pregnant by a miracle because she was old and should not have been able to have a baby. God had also sent an angel to Zachariah, Elizabeth's husband, to tell him that he and Elizabeth would have a son and his name would be John. When he grew up, people would call him John the Baptist.

This was a fulfillment of a prophecy from long before that John would baptize and preach to everyone that the Savior was coming. That Savior was the baby that Mary was going to have. John would be Jesus' cousin.

When Elizabeth heard Mary coming, the baby John leapt in her belly and together they knew that Mary's baby would be the Savior of the world.

December 7

WHERE DID JOSEPH LIVE?

The Bible tells us that Joseph, who became Mary's husband, lived in an area called Judea. To be safe after Jesus was born Joseph took his family to live in Egypt for a time. Then they moved to Nazareth where Jesus grew up.

We know that Joseph, the father who raised Jesus, was a carpenter. Carpenters make furniture and donkey carts that can be pulled, and shelves and many other things from wood. So we can imagine that Joseph lived in a house that was common for his time, and one that was probably near his wood shop where he worked.

December 8

WAS JOSEPH JESUS' FATHER?

We know that God was the heavenly father who created the miracle of birth through Mary. So we know that Joseph was not his birth father. But when the angel came to Joseph and told him to take Mary as his wife, he knew that he would raise and protect the baby as his very own. Joseph became Jesus' earthly father and like a child who is adopted, Joseph loved Jesus as if he were his very own son.

December 9

Why Did Joseph and Mary Go to Bethlehem?

When Joseph and Mary lived, the nation that ruled far and wide was Rome. The emperor was Caesar Augustus. Caesar wanted to know how many people there were in his whole kingdom so decided to count them all. To do that, all the people were ordered to go to the town where their family originally came from. Joseph's family was originally from the area of Judea and the town of Bethlehem. So that is where they went to be counted. Several hundred years before Joseph and Mary went to Bethlehem, there was a prophet named Micah. Micah received a message from God that the one who would someday be the ruler of all Israel, the one who would save everyone, would come out of Bethlehem. This was so surprising to everyone because Bethlehem was just a small town that no one really thought much about and no one would have thought that the Savior of the world would come from there. If Caesar had not wanted to count everyone, Jesus would have been born in a whole different place and the prophecy of Micah would not have been true. God moved everything to happen just as he planned from the beginning, and Joseph and Mary went to Bethlehem just at the right time in history.

December 10

Why Was There No Room in the Inn?

The emperor, Caesar Augustus, wanted to know how many people there were in his whole kingdom. So, he ordered that everyone far and wide in his whole Roman kingdom should go to their own hometown to be counted.

Bethlehem was a small town and was not used to having a lot of people come there all at the same time. There were not very many inns or hotels there. But since the order from Caesar said that everyone needed to go to their hometown to be counted, many people that had originally come from Bethlehem and the surrounding area arrived at the same time. They filled up all the inns where visitors could stay. By the time that Mary and Joseph got there, every place was filled up. There were no more rooms available.

December 11

What Did the Stable and Manger Look Like?

Everyone knows from Christmas songs that baby Jesus was wrapped tightly in swaddling clothes which are like warm blankets and then laid in a manger after he was born. But what is a manger? A manger was a large basket or box. Hay and other food was put in the manger and the animals like donkeys and horses could eat out of it. People think that it was probably made of wood with legs that held it up. You can imagine Mary arranging the hay to form the bedding for baby Jesus to lay in.

Some say the stable, where the manger was and where the animals were kept was a wooden hut or building like a barn. Others say that it might have been a cave. Whichever it was, it was probably the last place that Mary and Joseph thought that Jesus would be born. But even that was part of God's plan.

December 12

How Could a King be Born in a Stable?

How could it be God's plan that Jesus would be born in a stable. Did God make a mistake? We all can agree that a stable where animals live is the last place that a king would be born. Kings have the best of the best at birth and all of life. Mary and Joseph knew that baby Jesus would someday be king and savior of the world. Yet, there they were in a stable, the only place left where they could stay when they arrived in Bethlehem. This is truly an amazing part of God's plan!

In Heaven, Jesus was with God and had all the riches imaginable. So when he was on earth, the earth's riches seem pale and worthless in comparison. Jesus had a lot of work to do in his life when he grew up and he never valued money, jewels or gold or any of the things that we think are precious and valuable. What Jesus valued more than anything were the people like you and me. By Jesus being born in a humble stable, he showed the world even from the very beginning what is important and what is not.

December 13

WHAT DID MARY AND JOSEPH DO WHEN JESUS WAS BORN?

The bible does not tell us too much about the actual birth of baby Jesus. Mary would have felt what we call birthing pains that let her know that baby Jesus was almost ready to be born. Joseph was there with her and maybe he ran into the town and asked for help. Maybe there was a midwife there who knew about babies and giving birth. Maybe that is where the swaddling clothes came from. It was common in those days to have a midwife to help when babies were born. The bible does not talk about that part though. When Jesus was born, Joseph and Mary must have looked at his tiny face, hands, feet and his tiny body and praised God. To have a child, a boy, was a great gift at any time. To have a child that was directly sent from God was a true miracle. Mary and Joseph no doubt cried with joy and relief that after everything they had been through, they were safe and warm in that stable when Jesus was born.

December 14

Why Did They Call Him Jesus and Immanuel?

The birth of Jesus was the fulfillment of prophecies. These prophecies were revelations from God and given to us, to all people in the past and to us today, through His chosen prophets in the time before Jesus was born. When these prophesies were shared, they reassured and reminded people that God has a plan to remove the sin that came into the world through Adam's mistake in the Garden of Eden. This plan would restore all people who believed back to a relationship with God of love and everlasting life.

In the prophecies, this plan would be carried out by Immanuel, which in English means "God with us." The name Jesus is an English version of the original name as well. Another version of his name is Joshua, which means "The Lord is Salvation" (reminding us of Messiah, Savior). Names had special meanings especially back in that time. So, this baby that would someday save the world and be king was called, The Lord is Salvation or Joshua, our Jesus, and God with us, or Immanuel in the languages of history.

December 15

How Could There Be One Special Star for Jesus?

When we look in the sky there are so many stars and planets. Some are brighter than others. Sometimes we can see what looks like a star falling or shooting through the sky. The bible tells us that when Jesus was born a star appeared in the sky that was different from all the rest, so different that it drew particular attention to itself. There was an ancient prophecy about this star as well, and in a faraway land there were wise astronomers who knew about the prophecy and the star and about the coming Savior and King. When they saw the star, they knew immediately what it meant. It was the sign they had been looking for. The one that the prophecy foretold long ago had come into the world. The star that God put in the sky to announce to everyone who knew what to look for, that his Son had been born.

December 16

Where Did the Shepherds Come From?

The bible tells us about the shepherds that came to visit baby Jesus on the night he was born. These shepherds were Hebrews, Jewish people that were the descendants of Abraham. All the Jewish people at that time followed the Jewish law that was given to Moses directly from God hundreds of years earlier. They learned about the coming Messiah, someone that would change their lives forever by setting up a new good kingdom. He would be their Savior and they always looked towards his coming someday.

Shepherds were the ones that took care of herds of sheep and goats for the people. There were so many sheep and goats that they had to go far out in the fields to find the grass they needed to eat and water they needed to drink. The shepherds would move the herds of sheep from place to place every day and at night they camped out with the sheep to protect them.

December 17

How Did the Shepherds Know About the Birth of Jesus?

On the night that Jesus was born, the same night that the star appeared, some shepherds were camping out in the fields with their sheep to protect them as they always did. But on this night something very different and magical happened. An angel appeared right in front of them, surrounded by the glory of the Lord which must have looked like a great sparkling light. It frightened the shepherds so much. But the angel, who some believe was Gabriel the mighty angel of God, told them, "Don't be afraid! I am bringing you great news for all the world. Today the Messiah, the Savior you have been waiting for has come. You will find him as a baby, wrapped in blankets and lying in a manger in Bethlehem, the city of David." Then immediately the whole heaven was filled with angels singing and praising God. Their song was, "Glory to God in the highest and peace on earth to all those on whom his favor rests." Then they disappeared and the night was dark as it was before. The shepherds were so excited, they ran to Bethlehem and indeed found the baby lying in a manger and told Mary and Joseph and all they met what had happened and what the angel told them.

December 18

What Did the Angels in the Heavenly Host Look Like?

On the night of Jesus' birth, after the angel Gabriel gave the shepherds his message, many, many angels, appeared in the sky over the field. But what did they look like? Gabriel is called an archangel a chief heavenly servant of God. His appearance is described as looking like a man dressed in white clothing, but gleaming like the gem topaz and bronze, his eyes flaming and with a voice that sounded like a chorus.

To appear right in front of the shepherds at night must have been awe inspiring. Then after he gave his message to the shepherds, the sky was filled with a heavenly host of angels. Imagine the whole sky lit up with beings from heaven praising God in a language that the shepherds could understand. Since the sky was lit up, we can imagine that the angels were full of light like Gabriel but probably not so big or overwhelming. However, in that huge choir they must have looked and sounded beautiful. They praised God in their joy and excitement for what He was doing for the world. You can be sure that the shepherds remembered that night for the rest of their lives and told everyone they knew about it.

December 19

WHERE DID THE WISE MEN COME FROM?

Hundreds of years before Jesus' star appeared in the sky, a prophecy about the star was told. A prophecy is given from God to people to tell what he is doing or is going to do. There were certain people who lived far away from Bethlehem who studied the prophecies and the stars. We call them the wise men and they are famous in our Christmas story. Some people think that they were kings as well.

The bible tells us that they came from the east. There are many countries east of Bethlehem that these wise men could have come from. They could have come from Asia or India, even Egypt. But they came together so must have known each other and must have studied the stars together to know what this one special star meant to the world.

December 20

How Did the Wise Men Know to Follow the Star to Find the Baby King?

Through the ages there were astronomers who lived in the east, far away from where Jesus was born. They studied the stars and the prophecies. Each generation passed on to their children what they learned about how the stars moved in the heavens. One prophecy was about a special new star that would appear when a king would be born that would one day rule the world, conquer evil and bring good. When these astronomers finally saw this unusual star appear, they knew the promise had come. The prophecy told them that the appearance of the star meant the king had arrived. They knew that they had to start out towards Judah where the prophecy said the king would be. As they started out, the star moved before them and that confirmed what they had learned. The star brought them to the land where Jesus was born.

December 21

Why Was King Herod so Mad When He Heard About Baby Jesus?

At the time that Jesus was born, there was a king over the Jewish people. His name was Herod. Herod was allowed to be king as long as he obeyed the emperor, Caesar Augustus, who ruled over most of the known world at that time.

The wise men finally arrived in Judah after following the star all the way from their homes in the east. They went to the palace where Herod lived because they thought surely this king would be born in a palace. They asked Herod about the new baby king that was born. But King Herod did not know anything about this other baby that would be king. He got very jealous thinking that there was someone else that would take over as king, and he got mad. So he made a plan to get rid of baby Jesus.

December 22

How Can Jesus be from Bethlehem, Nazareth, Egypt and Galilee?

When people talked about Jesus, some would say he was from Nazareth, others would say Galilee, a prophecy said he came out of Egypt, and we know he was born in Bethlehem. How can Jesus be from all these different places? We know that Mary and Joseph came from the area of Nazareth and traveled to Bethlehem and that is where Jesus was born. So, when Jesus grew up, it was known that he started his life in Bethlehem. But when King Herod found out that there was a baby born somewhere in his country that would be king, he decided to kill all the babies that had been born at that time. An angel came to Joseph and warned him about King Herod's plan. So, Joseph took Mary and baby Jesus to Egypt for a few years until the danger had passed. When it was safe again, Joseph and Mary brought their baby back to Nazareth, their hometown. That is where Jesus grew up. So that is why we see that Jesus came from all of these places. He lived in each one and came from them, Bethlehem, Egypt, Nazareth, and Galilee.

December 23

WAS JESUS RICH?

Jesus was born into Joseph and Mary's life. Joseph was a carpenter and he most likely learned this from his father in a family business. While growing up in Nazareth as a carpenter's son, Jesus learned the trade as well. They were not rich but also not poor.

After Jesus grew up, he started telling people the good news that God was fulfilling the promises he made through his prophesies. Jesus told the people that God had sent him into the world to find and save the lost. He walked from town to town telling everyone about this. Jesus healed many people and gathered followers who believed his message. During all this time Jesus had no money of his own and took nothing with him. His followers supported him and wanted as many people to hear him as possible.

But the rest of the story is that Jesus was and is a true King. God in heaven owns all the riches imaginable and as God's own son, Jesus also owns all of that. So, while Jesus was here, he knew that true riches were not here on earth. What we call riches are nothing in comparison to the riches that are in heaven. So, yes, Jesus was rich, rich beyond measure, but had nothing to call his own while he was here on earth.

December 24

Did Jesus Know He Was the Son of God and not of Joseph?

Joseph and Mary knew the truth about who the real father of Jesus was. A few others did as well. But most people did not. Joseph raised Jesus as his own son and loved him. As a Jewish boy, Jesus went to school and learned the law of Moses and about the prophecies, even the prophecies that spoke of the coming Savior of the world, the Messiah. As Jesus grew older his true father, God, became known to him. We know this because one day when Jesus was 12 years old, Joseph and Mary were walking home from their annual trip to Jerusalem for the Passover feast. They thought that Jesus was behind them walking with his friends. But when they looked for him they could not find him. They became worried and went back to Jerusalem. They finally went to the temple, and there was Jesus, talking with the Jewish teachers about the law and the scriptures. Everyone was amazed at what Jesus knew at 12 years old. Joseph and Mary were so relieved when they found Jesus and started to scold him for causing such worry. But Jesus told them, "Don't you know I must be about my father's business?" At this, Joseph and Mary knew that Jesus was talking about his father, God in heaven.

December 25

When Was Jesus' Real Birthday?

We celebrate the birth of Jesus every year on December 25. It is always such a magical time of year. But was Jesus really born on that day?

We do not actually know what day Jesus was born because it was so long ago and the people of that day used a different calendar and a different way of marking time and events. We don't even know if they celebrated birthdays at all. But we do know that Jesus was born and that is great cause for celebration! So, hundreds of years ago, the date of December 25 was chosen and that is the day we look forward to every year to remember the birth of Jesus.

May you never lose your wonder and curiosity about Jesus, the life he led, the life he leads now, and the life to come. And keep all these things in your heart.

MERRY CHRISTMAS!

www.ingramcontent.com/pod-product-compliance
Lightning Source LLC
LaVergne TN
LVHW051040070526
838201LV00066B/4872